THE

Nita Joe

PROJECT
A JOURNEY OF HEALING

NaDonna Gary

ISBN: 978-0-578-80352-4

The Nita Joe Project

Proudly self-published through Divine Legacy Publishing, www.divinelegacypublishing.com

Dedication

Dear Momma,

I loved you then, I love you still, and I will love you always. There is not a day that goes by that I do not think about you and miss you. The sacrifice in all of this was to give a voice to the voiceless, freedom to those captive to hurt and fear, and peace to those in pain. But most of all healing!

Dear Christine,

I hope to live a life where you can follow in my footsteps, but I never want you to walk a day in my shoes.

My prayer is that my sacrifices afford you a life free from fear. I want you to know that. despite the mistakes of your parents, you are not bound to them, you are enough, and you are loved!

To the little girl who sits in the background watching her every move, copying her grace in the mirror, waiting for your day to be noticed as a woman, I see you!

To the woman who never got a chance to be that innocent little girl, I see you too. I have wept for you, I pray for you, I speak for you, and I dance for you. Today God gives you permission to hope for your future and freedom from your past. Today is your day to live!!

Preface

All my life, I have tried to put myself in the background because of fear. I limited myself to being average. I remember one day walking with my mother, and I asked her if she would be mad if I didn't get good grades on my report card. She said as long as it wasn't an F. I said, what about a C? She replied, "No, that's average. I was average in school, so I don't expect you to be anything less than average; I don't want you to do anything less than I did."

From that point forward, the bar was set. I proclaimed "average" as my goal. Now, I do not want to come off as if I am bashing my mom because I am not. I loved her very much; she was my "She-ro." To me, she was the most beautiful, graceful, funny, yet serious woman in the world. I used to cling to her every word. Once I asked, "Momma, will there be houses in heaven?" "Yes," she said. "And I hope there is wrestling too!" I loved when she was silly; I loved when she was stern. I just loved my momma. I wanted to be like her; dress like her, be pretty, funny, and full of life… just like her. So, if "average" was good enough for her it was even better for me. She was the first person I loved, the first person to love me, the first person to disappoint me, and the first person to leave me. My mother, in her way, taught me so much about life before I ever got a chance to live.

This is in dedication to Anita "Nita Joe" Gary: my mother, who died in 1997 from a heart attack and a stroke because of a long battle with drug abuse. This project is for women who have struggled emotionally, spiritually, physically, and financially, for the daughters of drug and alcohol abusers, domestic violence survivors, and those who have been labeled to have "mommy issues." My prayer for this project is faith-building, restoration, and empowerment. My vision as given to me by God is to have at least 90% of the women who complete the program have a closer relationship with God, a greater knowledge of survival, and freedom!

Most of us have heard the phrase "welcome to the 1st day of the rest of your life." Well, this is it! At this point you have decided two things: 1) I want to make a change in my life and 2) I want to be a better me. Congratulations, you made the first step! It takes 21 days to develop a habit, so each phase is broken down into 21 days of intense, extensive prayer, training, and support. This 63-day program consists of three phases. Each phase is designed to purposely break you down, build you up, and set you free. This project is not meant to be a magical system to fix your life in 63 days, however, you cannot fix what you will not face. The results are not cookie cutter. What works for one may not work for all, but this project is designed to help make you aware of your hindrances, face them, and take back control of your life with the help of God and your support system.

Anita vs. Nita Joe

Sunday, May 4th, 1997, will forever be a date etched in my mind. That was the day Anita Monae Gary left this earth. Although this was the date of her physical death, Anita Monae left long before then. The woman I had been living with was Nita Joe.

Anita, my grandmother's only child and her father's firstborn, was raised by my great grandmother Ernestine (MeMa as I call her). MeMa ruled with an iron fist, lots of prayers, and the fear of God. Although MeMa was tough, she could not contain the wildflower that was Anita Monae. Anita Monae was on a search to find that missing part. She wanted love. Birthed to teenaged parents, she was left behind as they went out in the world to become their own people. This search to find love would send her on a journey across miles from Memphis to Chicago, DC/Maryland, and back to Memphis. A journey of highs and lows, triumphs, and defeat. I would like to think my brother and I are a least two of those triumphs.

As I mentioned earlier, the spirit of my mother Anita left long before her physical death ever took place. Though I can't give a date, time, or even a year, in what seemed like a moment, Anita went from "momma" to "Nita Joe." For as long as I can remember, my momma smoked weed. It did not bother me; she seemed to enjoy it and it made her clean the house fast. After a while, it just became the fragrance of the house. Weed, Money House Blessing spray, and good vibes became my norm at home. Aside from her weed habit, she still managed to balance me, work, and even sang in a gospel group for a while. Life was good; it was just us. She would always tell me, "I don't care if we have to eat beans out of a can; it's going to be me and you." That's how it was, just me and my momma. Before she got a bed, we made a pallet and slept on the floor together. We celebrated when she got enough money to buy her new bed!

But such as life goes, things change. Before my mom met my stepdad, she had a few different boyfriends who came through and did some damage on the way out. For most of my childhood, my mom dated Anthony. He was always nice to me, and we never had any problems, until one night my mom was working, and I was home with the sitter. My mom told me on the phone that I could not sleep in her bed, but I was scared of the Gremlins movie poster in my room! After my bath I got in my bed,

I laid there until the sitter was asleep and I snuck in my mom's got into bed. I hid under the covers and tried to stay real still until I fell asleep. I felt someone get in the bed, I thought it was my mom. Suddenly, I felt hands on my butt. Then hands started to take off my panties. I jumped up, and it was Anthony! I ran to my room, scared and hiding. I vividly remember being scared! But I was so worried about being in trouble for sleeping in her bed, that I did not understand what had happened to me.

The next day, at MeMa's house, I told her what Anthony had done and, of course, she went off. She gave my mother a scolding and then my mom came to me. She told me that he wasn't trying to do it. That he thought it was her lying in the bed. I took her word for it, but I would never be the same again. The incident made MeMa double down on being strict and made me extra sensitive about my body. When I went to Chicago that summer, Grandma told me that MeMa had made me "scared of men" and that everyone was not out to hurt me. Soon after, momma and Anthony took a break and she met Larry. My mom met Larry when he was doing some work on MeMa's house. They seemed to hit it off well, however, things quickly turned bad and they broke up. After their breakup, he started doing all sorts of strange things. One day, when we were leaving the house, we came out to find he had slashed her tires. Another day, I was at school and the counselor came to get me from class. She took me to her office, and I was met by a lady from Child Protective Services. She asked me a bunch of questions about my mom to see if I was being abused at home. After telling my mom what happened at school, she told me that Larry had reported it.

After so many incidents, my mom ended back with Anthony. As we slept one night my mom heard a noise in the attic. I heard yelling coming from her room, so I went to investigate. When I got to her room she and Anthony were yelling and rushing to the front door. Larry was up in the attic and had drilled a hole in the ceiling over her bedroom to spy on her! Momma grabbed her gun and we all ran outside. We saw a man running down the street. She was sure it was him and began to shoot down the street! I was standing right in front of her as she did it. Anthony disappeared after that.

When I was in the second grade, things began to change again. The fragrance of the house changed, the vibe changed, and the company changed. Slowly, I was losing my Mommy, and Nita Joe was taking over. It was also in the second grade, in Ms. Lott's class at Gordon Elementary, when I committed the ultimate black family betrayal. I told my momma's business outside my house! I didn't mean to hurt my momma, and I definitely wasn't gossiping about her, but my momma was changing and I didn't know what to do. So, I went to the one person who was relatable at the time, my teacher, and told her to help. Well, that backfired on me very quickly! That afternoon, I got the scolding of my life right outside the house, and I was quickly reminded that, "WHAT GOES ON IN THIS HOUSE, STAYS IN THIS HOUSE!" So, we never spoke about it again, and it remained our family secret.

As time went on, my mommy, Anita, slowly began to fade away. Soon she met the man who would become my stepfather and became pregnant with my baby brother. Things were calm during her pregnancy, with no fragrance, but the company was different. To paint the picture for you, this was the late 80's. Crack was booming, and my new family was full of hustlers. Life around me began to move fast after my brother was born. As

Momma changed, I began to change too. My innocence was gone. I no longer had time to be a little girl, and it was time to grow up. When I fully understood that my mom was having a baby, I was excited! I was going to have a little sister. We were going to do everything together. I was going to take her to the mall and do her hair; my life-size doll! My momma promised me a sister, and I could not wait for her to arrive!

I spent that summer in Chicago with my grandmother. If I could have flown the plane home myself, I would have because I was ready to see my sister! I got home, and it was a boy! A cute curly head baby boy, but a boy! I was disappointed, but little did I know that would only be the first of many. Although I was not happy about my new little brother, he quickly began to grow on me. I took my role as big sister very seriously. My mom told me again, "I don't care if we have to eat beans out of a can; it is going to be us, me, you, and your brother." When my brother was younger, he had a few health problems. The biggest one was asthma. Before discovering this, he got very sick. What we then thought was a bad cold took a turn for the worse. I remember my mom speeding to the hospital, and I held him in my arms to keep him from crying. Suddenly, he stopped breathing. I yelled at my mom, "he's turning blue!" We got him there just in time to get him on a breathing machine. He spent a week in the hospital hooked up to all kinds of machines. I had never been so scared in my life. I think I prayed harder than I had ever done in my nine years on earth. From that moment on, I made it my mission to protect him with all the power I had.

As more time passed, things progressively got worse. When I was in the fourth grade, "what goes on in our house" began to find its way outside more and more. My mom and my stepdad started fighting all the time, physically, and her little habit was now a full-blown addiction. Her first attempt at gaining control was to go to rehab. Her check-in day was one of the saddest days of my life, or so I thought at the time. MeMa, Uncle Clarence, and I drove my mother to the hospital. We were all silent in the car, which was rare for my family—what usually was a five-minute drive seemed like five hours. I was losing my love for a drug, and I didn't understand why. Nita looked out the window the whole time, and she did not look at me because she was not ready to explain why she wasn't going to be back for a while. When we pulled up, she got out and simply said, "Mommy will be home soon" then, she turned and walked away. I sat there and watched her until I couldn't see her anymore. Two weeks later, she was home. I was happy to see her but disappointed. This wasn't Anita! She was still Nita Joe! And she wasn't better at all; she was worse. Anita Monae was gone. Nita Joe had run off with my mother. Although this seemed to be a considerable devastation to me at that moment, it was only the beginning of the roller coaster ride of drama and emotion that awaited me over the next six years preceding her death.

As Nita Joe began to take over more and more, so did the world around me. Her addiction became more of a priority, and things like her job and the light bill became less critical. After skipping out on light bills and car notes, rent began to fall behind and, eventually, we had to move out of our family home. Things were bad, but I didn't know how bad things were until my mom moved to Florida. If someone were to ask me when I first experienced loss, it would have to be Nita's move to Florida. It would be four years later when I found out the real reason why she left. But at the time, it felt like the first death. I do not remember her sitting me down to explain it. I do not even remember her saying goodbye. All I remember is, she was gone. My home was gone, and my family was separated. In the 5th grade, my grades were slipping, and I acted out with MeMa and did not know why. One Sunday, I was scared as hell because Uncle Clarence was coming over after church, and he was going to whoop me. MeMa rarely whooped me after Nita left. She always called Uncle Clarence for that; he was my uncle, but he was a father figure and discipline was his thing with me.

I was terrified of my uncle; MeMa used to say, "ain't no whooping like when God whoop you!" And I would think if God whoops you anything like Uncle Clarence, I need to do right! So yeah, I was scared! I didn't have any real reason for my behavior, and I knew I deserved that whooping, but I sure did not want it. I went to church, and I prayed not to get my butt torn up when Uncle Clarence got there. I should have realized then God was awesome because instead of my uncle putting me over his knee, he talked to me. That was one of the most real moments of my life because my uncle understood me.

He said to me, "I understand that you are acting out because your mama is gone, but you have to do better." And suddenly, MeMa burst into tears! She looked up and asked, "Is my living in vain? Is all of this in vain?" Her tears shook me! I had never seen MeMa cry outside of the church. I hugged her and cried with her. I told her I apologized, and I would do better. I was confused, sad, and mad all at once. But I could not express it to anyone, and for the first time, I taught myself how to be numb.

Numb feels good in the moment, but it is a scary place to be, especially for a child. Numb can cause you to block out things mentally to cope with your reality, but those memories and feelings can pop back up in the most inopportune times in your life. But there I was, numb and seemingly resilient, adjusting to life without my mother as I continued through my academic year.

It was summer, and Nita was back! She found a place within walking distance from MeMa, so I got to visit her on the weekends during the day, but I could not spend the night. Weekends at Nita's house were fun! I got to see my brother, I got to play outside with my friends and cousins all day, and most of all, I got to spend time with my mom. After a while, weekends were not enough; I wanted to spend the whole summer with her. That was the first summer I was not going to Chicago. MeMa was upset that my grandmother didn't send me a ticket, but I was happy because that meant I could spend the whole summer with my mother. Although MeMa was not happy about it, she still let me visit, but I still had to go home every Saturday night to go to church on Sunday. I was glad about it!

This new place was different. It was a two-bedroom shotgun duplex with the bathroom in the back of the house right off the kitchen. My room was set up, but we all slept in my Momma's room because that is where the TV and air conditioning was. It had a bad mice problem; that was one of the reasons why MeMa would not let me stay overnight at first, but Nita got it under control. She bought a cat named Noony and reported the landlord to the health department so that he would do repairs. But despite our sub-par living arrangement, I was happy because I was with my momma! I didn't ask her questions about why she had left or what she did while she was there. I was just happy she was back, we were together, and I didn't ever want to be away from her again.

But this new start came with a new set of problems. Things were different, I was different, the numb state wasn't really working anymore, and my emotions were all over the place. I couldn't explain it or even tell anyone what I was feeling; it would just come out in different ways. For instance, one evening, I was outside playing and the streetlights came on, which meant it was time to go inside. I went in, but no one else was home. I walked all through the house, calling names, but no one was there. When I realized I was by myself, I freaked out! I started crying uncontrollably, stomping, and screaming to the top of my lungs, "I WANT MY MOMMA!!!" In the middle of my breakdown, in walked Nita trying to figure out what was wrong with me. After calming me down, she asked me what was wrong, and I said, "I thought you were gone." She replied so simply, "I just walked to the store." I had spiraled at ten years old because my momma had walked to the store. After that little episode, we never talked more about it, and she did not explore my feelings or try to explain why. We just went on with life.

Things were calm for a while, and I had a chance to be a kid, go outside, ride my bike, hang with my friends, just regular, summertime, kid stuff. However, my summer bliss did not last long. It was early in the morning, and I woke up to arguing; my mom and my stepdad were fighting again. I did not know why they were fighting, all I knew was to be ready! When he hit her, I hit him. I got in the middle, trying to get him off of her. This fight went down the hall and to the front door. As he pushed her out the door, I was in the middle; my arm was somehow stuck in between her the door and him. The harder he pushed, the more pressure I felt on my arm, and then I felt a stain, and I screamed, "STOOOOP!!! My ARM!"

That scream was the only thing that stopped the fight. They both rushed to check on me, but I left. I walked to MeMa's house, tired, angry, and defeated because I knew my summer was over, and she was going to make me stay. When I got there and told her what happened, she was upset. She made me go into the house and stay, and just like that, my summer at my momma's house had come to an end.

Although I was safe at MeMa's house, I was not happy, and I made it known. MeMa's house was boring; she wouldn't let me leave the porch or the yard, I didn't have any friends over there, my only fun was going to church, and on top of all of that, I started my period! In my ten years of life, this had to be the worst summer ever. With my emotions all over the place, I was not the best version of my ten-and-a-half years of life; that had to be the worst summer ever! One day MeMa made me mad about something. I can't remember what it was, but I knew I wanted my momma, so I snapped. There in the driveway, I had a full breakdown, and I wasn't going to get a switch or strap to get a whooping. That day I was fed up! I went into full panic mode, heavy breathing, crying, screaming, and then I ran! I ran to momma's house because she would save me from whatever it was MeMa wanted to do. I was wrong. That protest did not last long, and I was right back at MeMa's house, and the reinforcements had stepped in. Cousin Jackie was there, we all were on the porch, and she asked me one question, "Do you want to come to stay with me?"

I entered sixth grade living with Cousin Jackie. It was another move, a new school, and a whole new mix of emotions. It was different there, but peaceful. I had two cousins there close to my age, so it wasn't bad, but It still wasn't home. I wasn't with my momma. This was a punishment, and I felt like this was repayment for acting out with MeMa. I was in many extracurricular activities living with Cousin Jackie, which made coping with not being with my mom a little easier. We did cheer and dance class, and we had a big end of the year recital. I was so excited and nervous most of all because my mom was coming! She came, and after the recital, she bought us all pizza, and I got a chance to go home with her… for good.

The Beginning of the End

Things seemed to be on the right track. I was living with my mom in a new place. This was a new beginning. Things were different in the new place; there were a lot of kids my age. I was meeting new people and things were cool. For the first time in two years, I enjoyed living life with my mom, and she seemed to be doing better. We were a family again. But, as my life pattern was going, this new beginning would come with a whole new set of problems. The four years that followed were the beginning of the end. It was my first year of junior high, another new school, and a new part of town. Nita wanted me to go to this "good school," so she used a friend's address and enrolled me halfway across town. We did not have a car at that time, so I would be taking the bus alone. The new school was cool. It was a long bus ride, and I had to leave extra early to make it there on time.

On my first day, I was scared as heck. Luckily, my neighbor was a senior at the high school nearby, so he let me walk to the bus with him and taught me the bus route. This new school was challenging, but I liked it. Especially in my English class. That teacher helped me discover a passion for writing. She took an interest in me; she helped me develop as a writer and gave me confidence! She even entered me into an oratorical contest at school. Though English was great, I struggled at this school, mostly because of the long commute and struggled to get to school on time. I was suspended several times for tardiness, and as a result, I failed the seventh grade. I was spending summer in Chicago with my grandmother when I received that news.

Summer ended abruptly. Nita transferred me to my neighborhood school, Humes Jr. high school, for seventh grade, the sequel. Humes was much different from my previous school. My friends from the neighborhood went there, so it felt more like home. The sequel went well. Other than the normal teenage experience, life was chill for the moment. Things remained quiet… until eighth grade. Eighth grade started rough for me. Even though things were quiet on the home front, things could not be darker on a personal level. I was changing, my body was changing, and I did not like becoming a young woman. Most of the time, I wanted to be alone. I wore clothes twice my size to cover up my body, and I started smoking cigarettes, until my mom caught me.

Things with my mother's health started taking a turn for the worse. The drugs took a toll on her body, and she had her first heart attack, which resulted in me going back and forth between my house and my godmother's house. I entered the numb state again, and I could not explain to anyone what I was feeling. I dealt with it in all different ways, like skipping school and hanging out later and later that summer. I smoked weed with my friends. I lost my virginity and could not tell anyone, and I got my first summer job. My summer was busy with work and hanging with my friends, so it seemed to fly by. That year for my birthday in August, my mom decided to go all out. I was turning 15 and, for the first time, my mom let me have a sleepover! She let me go to a teenage club and even rented me a limo. That was the best birthday I had.

Ninth grade was a game-changer for me. It was my last year at Humes, and my class was the last ninth grade class before they moved it to the high school, so it should have been an exciting time. But it turned out to be less than great. The school year kicked off smoothly. School was fun! I was finally feeling good about myself as a young woman. I had a boyfriend. My summer job became my part-time job, letting me work during the school year. It finally felt like things were looking up for me. However, things on the home front were changing again. My mother and stepfather had reached a point where they were just roommates. He was cheating on her, and she was doing the same, but they would not separate because of my brother. We all co-existed together and tried to keep the peace, but that didn't last long. By then, I'd stopped getting in the middle of their fights unless things got out of hand.

My brother was getting older, so I tried to keep him from seeing some things, but that proved very difficult in our house. At the time, our house was what some in the hood would call "the lab" or "the trap." A lot of illegal activity went on there. My stepfather sold weed, and because he did not trust my mom, it was my responsibility to hold his stash. In addition to the weed stash, there were guns and other drug paraphernalia that helped aid the dealers in preparing and distributing their products. My mom worked nights as a bartender at this hole in the wall night club, so if someone needed to come "cook-up," I had to let them in and supply what they needed. I didn't get a lot of sleep, but that was our norm and our secret. There was never a dull moment, and life was a constant roller coaster of danger because, with every knock at the door, I never knew if it would be a robber, a junkie, or the police.

I was always on edge, and in the moments that I could find sleep, my dreams would haunt me. I spent a lot of time trying to stay away from home, physically and mentally. I was either out all day after school getting high with my friends or at my godmother's house. Weed was my mental escape, so when I went home, I could be numb and get a few hours of sleep before reality came knocking, literally. And it always did. and boy, did it knock loud! That same year in November, I remember sitting outside on the steps with my BFF Kaye when her mom came and pulled me to the side. She asked, "Do you want to come to stay with us?" I was puzzled she'd ask because we lived next door to each other. She saw my confusion and realized I did not know that my mom would be in jail for a while. She told me I was more than welcome to stay with her. I was very grateful to her for opening her home to me. And I was right back to being numb.

After that conversation, I went to talk with Nita. There was not much explanation, other than I would be going to live with my godmother. So that's where I went. I wasn't happy about it because I would be away from my boyfriend and friends, but I felt peace there because I could sleep. I had work and school to keep me busy most of the time, so I did not allow myself to feel anything. When Thanksgiving rolled around, though, it was weird to me. Out of all the times Nita went missing in my life, she had never missed a holiday, so her absence that year hit me like a ton of bricks. I was sad all that day. When it was time to eat, I was alone in my room crying. My godmother called me to the phone. It was Nita, and the first thing she asked when I got on the phone was, "You were crying, weren't you?" I answered yes, to which she replied, "I know because I felt it, and that is why I called." We had a strange bond like that; I could feel when something was wrong with her, and she could feel things with me. That phone call helped me get through my day, helped me get back to numb.

In December, my brother and I got a chance to visit her; she was at the Penial Farm. It seemed like we drove forever to get there, and then we had to stand in a very long line. When we finally got to the front of the line, the guard would only let family in, so my brother and I had to go in alone. I was nervous and excited all at the same time. I was ready to see Momma, but not in that place. We sat across from her, and she looked so good! She had her hair done and looked happy despite being behind bars. I remember asking her how she got her hair done, and I asked her if anyone was trying to harm her in there. She laughed at it off and said no, and we enjoyed the time we had left of our visit. Oddly, I left the visit in peace. I was more focused than I had ever been, and I was determined to make Christmas great for my brother. I was still working my after-school job, and I was saving my money, so I asked my godmother to take me to the store to buy him some things. I told her I could do without, but he is a kid, and he would not understand. Without hesitation, she took me, and I bought him everything that I could.

We continued to push forward. I was preparing my mind to spend my first Christmas ever without my mom when a miracle happened. Nita was released on Christmas Eve. When I got home that night, she was there. I heard the music playing as I came up the stairs. When I walked in, she was in the kitchen; it was grocery bags everywhere, Christmas decorations, and happiness. We may have stayed up half the night cooking and talking as a family, all of us! Even she and my stepdad were getting along. It was the best Christmas ever! It wasn't about the gifts; we were just happy to be together again. But this bliss did not last long.

Nita's health began to decline again. She was in and out of the hospital for various reasons until she was diagnosed with kidney failure. She was in hospital for weeks on end, and it was very painful to watch. Her hands and feet were swollen like balloons from retaining water. She was in so much pain. I remember rubbing her hands and feet, trying to relieve her, but it was only a temporary fix. She called me from the hospital one day and asked me what I would do if the doctor told her she had six months to live. I told her I didn't know. She got so upset with me. In her mind, I didn't care, but I was honestly numb and didn't know how to answer that. She was released from the hospital to start dialysis treatment. The first round of treatment did not go well because the trach in her arm was not working properly. Another week in the hospital, and she came home ready to get on track.

Nita and my stepdad had gone back to co-existing then. He had a girlfriend, and she had a boyfriend, but they still decided to stay in the same house. She just moved into the room with my brother and me. My brother had his bed, yet we all slept in the same bed together. I guess it made her feel closer to us. Soon, she was back to her old tricks, or at least she tried to be. One night I dreamt of her funeral. The dream scared me so bad I woke up and found her bent over the toilet, throwing up and sick. I asked, "What's wrong?" She answered, "I can't even get high anymore because it makes me sick." I angrily yelled, "GOOD! I hope it makes you sick every time it touches your lips!" After helping her off the floor, we sat down on the couch, and I told her, "I just dreamt of your funeral." She ominously replied, "You probably did." I told her not to speak like that.

The one consistent thing I had in my life has always been the church and my relationship with God. There are times in life that God is preparing you for something before you even know it's going to happen. Looking back, God had been preparing me for what was about to happen that night. That dream would be the first of many "strange things" that would prepare me for what was to come. As Nita continued to do her thing, I became more detached and angrier, and the stranger things got for me. Walking down the street was different for me because I would come across something dead everywhere I went. I remember being in the car with my godsister and seeing a dead squirrel in the street. I told her then I thought something is going to happen because I kept seeing dead stuff. Things only get stranger from here.

It was a Sunday morning when Nita woke me up to help find her shoes. Sleepy and irritated, I got out the bed and searched through the closet to get her gold J. Renee pumps to go with her emerald green suit and gold purse to match. As I went through the shoes with an attitude, Nita was in a joyful mood. She rambled on about how, when I was little, I loved to get her shoes for her and she kept asking me how she looked. She had sprained her ankle a week before that, so she had to walk around with an ACE bandage on, and it was messing up her outfit. She must have asked me five times did she look okay before finally getting ready. She had started attending a new church with an old friend of hers, and I was supportive because reading the Bible seemed to give her peace while taking her treatments.

After she finished her make-up, we talked a little bit before her ride came. I asked her if she was coming home that night, she said she would because she had dialysis the next morning. I gave her a few dollars to put in the collection plate, and I watched her and her friend drive away. I got ready for church like any typical Sunday and continued with my day. But church felt different that day. It was first Sunday, and everyone was there, even people that hadn't been there in a while. I remember wondering what was going on because there were just so many people at church that particular Sunday.

After church, sitting outside at home I talked with my neighbor, an older lady who lived downstairs. She was raising her grandchildren and loved to scrap and eat the ice out of our freezer! While sitting out there, everyone that passed kept asking me, where is your momma? My stepdad, my brother, even MeMa all asked. I told each of them the same thing, "She will be back tonight because she has dialysis in the morning." That day my neighbor shared why she was raising her granddaughters. She told me that their mom had been killed. I remember feeling sad that I couldn't imagine living without my mom. Then mt neighbor went inside, and I went upstairs and fell asleep.

Later that night, Kaye woke me up. I didn't think anything of it because she was pregnant and when she couldn't sleep, I would sit up with her. But this time was different. She would typically joke, but her mood was different as she told me to come back to her house. I had a phone call. We did not have a phone, and my godmother would call Kaye's house to get in touch with us. When I walked in the door, I heard her mom say something about the hospital, and I was instantly irritated because that meant Nita was sick again, and I was going to have to pack up and go to my godmother's house. When I got on the phone, it was Grand, my godmother's mom, who said, "Your momma is dead." I replied, "Quit playing with me" and dropped the phone, but Momma J assured me that it was not a joke and commanded me to pick up the phone.

When I put the phone back to my ear, her words fell on deaf ears; I could no longer hear anything she was saying. By the time she finished talking, my godsister and godbrother were coming to take me over to my godmother's house. I was frozen and in shock, and I started to cry. They told me to pack up; no one was home. When I went to pack a bag, I saw some of momma's belongings and had a meltdown. For the rest of the night, I kept hearing the gospel song "No cross, No crown" in my head. Numb.

The days leading up to the funeral were so long, and still, I wasn't ready. My friends from school came around to laugh and joke with me, but when I was alone, I cried when no one could see me. One minute, people told me you to cry and let it out, and the next they'd say to me not to cry. So, I swallowed most of my tears and remained numb until we had to write her obituary. We were all at MeMa's house sitting around the table getting the arrangements in order. My grandma sent me to the house to get pictures, and that is when everything went left. I had not been back there since the night she died, and I had mixed emotions about going in.

I walked up the stairs, went into the house, and went straight for the photo album, trying to avoid everything else. Then I went into our room. I went to the closet to look for some clothes, and all my stuff was gone! Everything was gone, her property, my stuff, everything. Then I turned and saw her purse from the hospital, and the walls came crashing down! It was like I had seen a ghost. I ran out of there so fast, and back to MeMa's house, they thought someone was chasing me. I must have looked like I had seen a ghost, too, because they all asked me what was wrong with me when I got back.

That same night, I had my first real cry in Joyce's hallway. I didn't sleep well that night. Every time I closed my eyes, I saw that gold bookbag purse. It was haunting me; I couldn't take it. I asked Joyce if I could sleep in her room. When she asked me why, I broke down. I told her about the purse, the house, and how my grandma looked so much like my mom, and I could not take it anymore. I could not make it through the night alone. I didn't know how I would make it through her funeral.

The day before the funeral, we had to view the body. I didn't know if I was ready for that, but I sucked it up and pushed through. Plus, I had to be strong for my brother. It was a long drive down to Mississippi. We walked in, and there she was, as if she were asleep. They said I had to do it. They told me I needed to look at her before we got to the funeral so that it wouldn't be any surprises. She'd had another heart attack and a stroke, so her face was a little distorted to the point that it looked as if she were winking at you. One of her best friends, Sylvia, did her hair and makeup. She had on a white slumber gown with pink roses to match the ones in the back of her casket and, for the first time in years, she looked like herself. She looked peaceful. That was what I wanted for her, but in life, not death. As I stood there and looked at her, I wasn't scared or sad; I too was at peace. We all sat there for a while in silence. Then my grandmother stood over her, fixed her gown, and made sure her hair was in place. She bent down to kiss her, and MeMa screamed, "Don't do it!" Grandma snarled back, "Why not?" as she proceeded with her goodbyes. MeMa's antics lightened the mood for a minute as we shared a laugh about old wives' tales, and we headed home.

The day of the funeral was beautiful; the sun was shining, and the weather was nice. We all met at MeMa's house before heading to the church. I was nervous and excited at the same time because all of my family would be there. It's crazy how funerals bring people together. For the first time in my life, I saw all of my family together in one place. Some of my mother's friends from DC came down with my grandfather, and it seemed like the whole neighborhood was there. It made me happy to see everyone come out to show their love. The church was packed with people, her service was going as usual, and I was holding up well until my Aunt Carolyn got up to sing "Amazing Grace." Don't get me wrong, she has a beautiful voice, but I was upset. After all, I had begged my Grandma not to have her sing that song because I knew it would break me! As soon as my uncle played that first note, the church was torn up.

As she began to sing, I ran out because I did not want to break down in front of all of those people. I went to the bathroom to cry. My godsister and brother followed me, and we all cried together. I told them my break down was about the song, but my reality was sneaking up on me to try to sucker punch me in the face. After my bathroom cry, I felt myself slip back into numb, and I pulled myself together enough to make it through the rest of the funeral. I use the word numb loosely in reference to times or situations where I went into a state of no emotion. However, retrospectively, some of these instances of numb were an exercise in experiencing grace.

Although I had been upset that my aunt chose to sing that song, God knew that I would need that grace to get me through the burial. This was our final goodbye. Even though I was not ready, it was happening, and I had no control over it. In my opinion, that was the worst part of the whole situation. There were so many missing pieces, unanswered questions, missed opportunities, and future experiences cut short, stuffed in a box, and lowered down in the dirt to be buried. Only grace and mercy had the strength to hold me together as I closed my eyes for a second, hoping that if I did not look, then maybe it wasn't real. But it was very real and final, and as quickly as I closed my eyes, it was over. I had to quickly throw on a smile and carry on with my day. In my 15-year-old wisdom laughing and joking was the best thing I could do to cope with all the heaviness of that day, so that's what I did. The repass was at MeMa's house; people were in and out eating and fellowshipping. My cousins, aunt, and I were hiding out chilling in MeMa's room, laughing and joking about things from the day.

My moment of laughter was quickly cut short as my grandma walked in, looked me straight in my eyes, and said, "Are you coming to live with me?" and proceeded to stare me down for the answer. I paused nervously to think because I had not thought that far ahead. My routine was to stay with my godmother when my mom was away, and I had plans to live with her before Nita died to get out of my old neighborhood and go to the high school near her. Moving to Chicago was never a presented option until that moment. As she impatiently waited for my answer, I nervously shrugged out a yes, to which she quickly snapped back, "Good. Because if you would have said 'no,' I was going to take you out of my will!" and she walked off. I sat there, confused about what I had just agreed to. I made a major decision about my life in a matter of minutes. While I sat trying to gather myself, my grandmother, in her true fashion, went to the porch where everyone was and made the announcement to my family. Everyone seemed happy except me, but I smiled and nodded then left with my sister and cousin. Nightfall made my reality hit hard. To help take the edge off, my sister and cousin decided we should smoke. However, smoking weed was not the same for me anymore because it made me go deep into thought, and that was the last thing I wanted to do. That would be the last time I smoked weed until I was in college.

The weeks following the funeral seem to run together, but I tried to enjoy the last of my time in school with all the ninth-grade activities and graduation coming up. My friends were a big help in keeping me company and helping me keep things off my mind. We hung out every day, and I spent as much time with them as I could before I had to leave.

As much as my mom and stepdad fought, I was surprised at how hard he took Nita's death. He started drinking a lot, not eating, and lost a lot of weight. On top of losing Nita, once my grandma made her decision that I was going back to Chicago with her, he thought that meant he would be losing my brother, too. Like my stepdad, I assumed that we both were going because Nita had always said she never wanted us to be split up. However, grandma told me that they sat down and talked, and she did not want to take his son away from him. Although he was pleased, it felt like another punch in the gut because I knew that was not what Nita would have wanted. I just thought it was wrong. I went to Chicago by myself.

Life After Death: The Chi-City Project

Nita died May 4th; her funeral was May 12th. I went to my freshman prom, finished the school year, and was in Chicago by Memorial Day. Separated from my brother, my friends, and my home, my whole little world was gone in an instant. It was almost as if someone snapped their fingers and the lights went out. The funny thing was, though, that amid all the noise I felt peace and relief. I was away from the neighborhood and away from the drama at my house. For the first time in a long time, I felt safe. It was a long summer, but I kept busy. I was not entirely new to Chicago because I spent almost every summer there since I was old enough to ride a plane by myself at five. And although this trip was different, I quickly fell into my normal summer routine. But I had my moments when I would cry alone in my room, making sure that no one could hear me. My emotions were all over the place some days. I was sad, numb, and mad all at the same time. But I kept it moving… until it was time to register for school. I was numb the whole day, my grandma and the school officials talked to me, but all I heard was "blah." I was there physically, but my mind was in a fog. I was having an out of body experience. Then reality hit. I was not going home!

Yes, I know she died. I went to the funeral. I watched her go in the ground and even visited her grave the next day on Mother's Day. But that, the moment was the most real thing I felt in months. Even though I had lived through all of that, my mind convinced me that I was going home at the end of the summer. Enrolling in school cleared the fog and shined a light on my reality. I WAS NOT GOING HOME! That night I cried my eyes out, hard, and fell asleep. I dreamt of my mom that night, and it felt so real. We were back home in the living room having one of our early morning talks in the dream. We were laughing and joking when I asked, "For real, Ma, why did you leave us?" She grabbed my hand, looked straight at me, and said, "I didn't leave you; I will never leave you." Then I felt her hand slip away. I felt a weight lift off the bed as if she had been sitting on it! That's how real it felt, as if she was really in my room and had come back to me. When I woke up, I sat up on the side of the bed and cried. That was the first time, since her death, that I allowed myself to grieve freely. I realized that she was gone, and I had to let her go. I was sad, but that moment gave me peace and a reason to keep going…

and I did. I went to school and faced that first day like so many others to come, with peace and protection.

Life with grandma was very different. It was quiet and more structured than life with my mom. Because my grandmother did not play a significant role in raising my mother, she decided to use the second chance to raise me. As a child, my mom would say I was grandma's favorite because we had a great relationship, and she always would buy me good gifts. She did try to spoil me, but it did not come without work. She planned to try to break all my "Memphis ways" and teach me how to adapt to life in Chicago. In my first year of high school, she shut down any extracurricular activities, and I could not go anywhere if it wasn't with my cousin. I never went to a football or basketball game in high school like other kids. If I was not doing chores or studying, I was just in my room. Sometimes, I would hang with my cousin, but she was a senior and getting ready to go off to college so, we couldn't hang as much. This new routine was very different for me because I was used to moving on my own and going as I please, but as my grandmother often reminded me, "You are not in Memphis anymore."

Everything with my grandma was a lesson. Before she began anything, she would say, "Come on, let me show you how to do this because don't no man want no woman who can't…" My love of cooking came from her because that is where she did her thing. That's where we bonded the most. My time in the kitchen with her prepared me for anything I would encounter with any chef in my future. She was very critical of everything I did, but out of love.

In my early teenage years, I was kind of tomboyish, so she was very critical about how I dressed and made me more aware of my body. For example, she told me to wear long skirts that hid my legs because I am "knock-kneed." She never owned gym shoes and few flats, so she rarely bought me any unless I needed them for gym. She was always on me about how I spoke because of my southern accent, so she suggested that I record myself and listen to how I talked to change it. She was a retired telephone operator, so speech was critical to her.

Almost every day after I finished my homework, I would go into her room, and we'd watch TV together and she had a story to tell me about her life. We could talk about almost everything except my mother. I better not ever had brought up my dad. I spent a lot of time with my grandmother, I enjoyed her company, and her approval was significant. She always pushed me to learn as much as I could about "handling business." She taught me how to write checks, pay bills for her, and every time she had to go into the bank or an office to meet with anyone, she made sure that I went with her and told the person that I was there to learn. She was always trying to prepare me for if something happened. She would say, "When I die, you might be sad, but you can cry those tears later; you make sure you handle your business first!" I used to think that she was so strong, so I used that advice for years as my go-to for strength.

Although I thought nothing could break her, I quickly learned that weakness comes in different ways for all of us. My grandma was sickly. She had over 21 surgeries, and as a result, she developed a slight addiction to pain medication. In her earlier years, she suffered from alcoholism, but the threat of losing her pancreas helped her get clean. During my high school years, she was pretty functional because she was very conscious of her image, so she did everything in a certain way so that if she were seen in public, it would appear what we call today, socially acceptable. She would tell me things like, "A lady never drinks out of a bottle, always pour your drink in a glass," and "never smoke in public." For the most part, she did an excellent job keeping her "little secrets" from me, except for that weed habit that she thought she was hiding from me. I would sometimes hear her up late at night, cooking in the kitchen. I could smell weed coming from her room; then, I would hear her spraying Money House Blessing air freshener. I, of course, was all too familiar with that combination. I never told her that I knew because I did not want to seem disrespectful.

After my mother's death, MeMa's mind began to get worse. On top of that, my grandma's brother Uncle Clarence's health took a turn for the worse, too. He died on New Year's Eve in 1997. Exactly six months after my mother died, we were right back at the same church having another family funeral. MeMa took his death hard, and what we thought was just old age and grief would send MeMa's "bad mind" into Alzheimer's disease. This added pressure on my grandma mentally and financially; she started traveling back and forth from Chicago to Memphis more. During this time, I saw some changes, but they were up and down. MeMa died in my junior year of college during finals week. We had her funeral on my mom's birthday. I had a mix of emotions behind MeMa's death. That was my girl. My heart. And although I did not like seeing her mind go, and I didn't want to see her suffering. I just never thought she would die. I don't know if I was numb or at peace, but my mind only would not allow that to be real. Even her funeral was a blur because, in my mind, it wasn't real. It didn't become real for me until three years later, when I went to Memphis and pulled up in her driveway to realize she was not there. I broke down in her driveway.

After MeMa's death, I began to see some changes in my grandma. Grief has a way of taking a toll on your entire body, especially if you are not fully prepared to deal with it. Looking back, I could not imagine being in her shoes. She lost a daughter without ever mending her relationship with her, she lost a brother six months after that, and then lost a mother after watching her battle a mental disease… all while battling her struggle with health, a secret addiction, and other demons she never told anyone. She kept going like normal, but after MeMa's death, things started to get progressively worse. Although MeMa's passing was a relief for her physically, mentally it took its toll. She blacked out a few times at MeMa's, and that resulted in a visit to a Neurologist.

We didn't talk as much when I was away at school, but when I came home during breaks, I started to notice little things like empty pints of liquor in the trash and large size PM pill bottles that she carried around in her purse. I became concerned when she came to visit me during Christmas break. She slept all day; I had to wake her up to eat, then she went right back to sleep. I even had to tell her to shower. That made me realize something was wrong, but she assured me she was fine. Of course, that wasn't true.

In January of 2005, I got a call that would change the course of my life for the next three years. She'd had a stroke and was hospitalized, and it was not looking good. When I got to the hospital, my grandma was awake and talking, but something different went on with her mind. Soon, they transferred her to a rehabilitation nursing facility, and I quickly realized that she would never be the same. I went back to school, dropped all my classes, packed my apartment up, and headed back home. After a few weeks, one of her nurses pulled me to the side and asked me about who would be able to care for her at home. When I told her it was only me, she looked me dead in the face, and she asked me. "Are you sure you want to do this? Because it is more than a notion." She advised me to put her in a permanent nursing home. But I couldn't do that. That was not what she would have wanted.

I didn't have any other options, so even though I didn't know what to do, I wrapped my head around being a full-time caretaker. We had to stay with my aunt for two weeks because we had to get the carpet taken up at home and get her hospital bed ordered. When Auntie Michele and I went to get her room ready for the hospital bed to arrive, we found evidence that her little habit had grown into a full-blown addiction. There were bags and bags of empty vodka and Excedrin PM bottles that she had hidden in the corners of her room or stuffed in purses in her closet. I got the real scope of what I was facing as a caretaker in our first week home. The first couple of months were hell because grandma was like a baby. The stroke had made her paralyzed on her left side, and she had dementia. It interfered with her speech; she could not feed, bathe, or dress herself and was very combative. We were on the way home from Auntie's house, and she asked me for a cigarette. I told her the doctor said she could smoke any more. She kept asking, and I kept telling her no, and she got agitated. She grabbed a hand full of my braids, wrapped them around her hand, and started pulling my her while I was driving! I had to restrain myself from reacting. I managed to pull the car over and got out quickly. After she calmed down, I got her home, and that night, I just cried in my room. I was 23 years old, and that was my new life.

It was rough adjusting at first. My friends were out living life, doing what 20-somethings do, and I was stuck at home. During this time, I went back to numb. It was my safe space, and soon it became my norm. But grandma was improving physically. She regained her ability to feed and bathe herself; she started to walk again with assistance, and her speech improved, but mentally she was never the same again. The neurologist prescribed medicine for her dementia, but he explained that should she never go back to her old self. The medicine was just to help slow the disease's progression and decrease her chances of having full-blown Alzheimer's.

After three years of being her caretaker, I decided to take back my life; there was nothing else could do for her. That was one of the hardest decisions of my life. I was torn between wanting a life for myself and not following her wishes of never wanting to be in a nursing home. I struggled with the decision for a while until Cousin David, one of my grandmother's first cousins who is like an uncle figure to me, gave me some advice that I still use to this day. He said, "Pray about it, and if after you pray if you feel peace with your decision, then that's the right decision to make." I did just what he said, and I decided that I had done all that I could do for her, and I wanted to figure out the rest of my life.

I found a place for Grandma and although I was scared and nervous, I knew she was safe and in good care. Then, I started my journey to culinary school. For two years I juggled work, school, and visiting grandma. I felt like I had to make up for the time I lost being at home and I often measured myself against the accomplishments of my friends, never feeling like I was doing enough. During my externship for culinary school, the restaurant that I was externing at offered me a job and I was finally breaking into my field. Things were busy, but I didn't complain. I was "at home" in the kitchen, so it didn't feel like work. But such as life goes, there was a turn of events that would change the course of my life again…

I always kept my phone near me when I slept at night because I never knew when I was going to get a call from the nursing home about Grandma. One night in particular, they had taken her to the ER for stomach pains and needed to keep her overnight for some observation. That overnight stay turned into a week and they sent her back to the nursing home. Before I could even find out that they released her, they were calling me again. They told me she had fallen, and they were taking her back to the hospital. That time it was a broken hip. Everything was happening so fast with her. Every time I got a chance to catch my breath, they called me about something else. After her hip surgery, the doctor wanted to meet with me.

I was nervous all that morning because I had no idea what they wanted to discuss. My sister went with me for support, and the nurses seated us. A team of doctors filed in like they were going to a press conference. They sat around the table silently, looking at my sister and me, and then the head doctor finally turned to me and asked, "Is there anyone else coming?" I told him, "No this is it." He then told me I looked too young to be making "this decision." After that statement, I knew that the meeting was about to go left. He went over my grandmother's chart, talked about her hip surgery, and stated that during surgery they found several other things that were more pressing than her hip. The pumping function of her heart was diminished, and her kidneys were functioning at a low rate. He went on to explain the risks of operating on her and he suggested that I sign a Do Not Resuscitate (DNR) form.

They dumped all of that information in my lap and filed out of the room as quickly as they came in. My sister and I said there for a minute as I tried to hold back tears. Then I went numb and quickly pulled it together because I had to go to work. I was so nervous and confused at that point because they were putting the decision about her life in my hands. I got to work and had a break down in my car. I could not understand why God would give this to me when I had no idea what to do and no time to figure it out. I cut that breakdown short and pulled it together enough to pray and go to work. The next day I signed the DNR, and they moved her to ICU to keep her on a ventilator. After Grandma spent a week in ICU, they called me back to the hospital. That time it was to meet with a hospice nurse. I went alone.

They sat me in a waiting room for that visit, so I was hopeful that things were going to be better, but it only got worse. The nurse walked in, sat quietly, and started going through the paperwork. After about a minute or so she looked up at me and as the doctor had, she asked, "Is there anyone else coming?" I told her no. And just like the doctor, told me I looked too young to be making this decision by myself. At that moment I sat up in my seat, took a deep breath, and said, "It's just me." She nodded and went on to explain to me what hospice was and that they had done all they could in ICU, but Grandma's situation wasn't getting any better and they were going to move her to the hospice floor to make her comfortable. When she was done, I nodded, told her to thank you, held in all my tears, and I went to work.

The next day was the meeting at the funeral home to go over her pre-arranged burial policy to make sure everything was updated, just in case. During my meeting, the nurse called and said, "You need to get here because I think she is about to take her last breath." I quickly hung up and raced to the hospital...but by the time I arrived, she was gone. That night I laid in bed way past Numb. I was just plain tired. I was too tired to cry. I was too tired to think. I knew I had no time to be sad. I put in my headphones, listened to some gospel music, and let the tears roll down my face. For the first time in two years, I turned off my phone and got some sleep.

Planning Grandma's funeral was different. Although I had been through that twice, I had been on the sidelines. For Grandma, I was really in the game. I had no time to be sad because it was all on me. I had to suck up the tears and "take care of business." I experienced God's grace at that moment because I wasn't sad; I was focused. Luckily for me, Grandma was a planner and she had specific things she wanted in a very specific way, down to the flowers. So, the most I had to do was go to places and sign papers, and for that I was grateful.

After grandma's death, I am still not sure if I was numb or just plain old tired. At the time, I was just out of culinary school and working two jobs. I had taken a few days off to handle the funeral, but literally, the day after I was right back to work, back to my normal routine, and grieving took a back seat once again.

After some of the smoke cleared, I took an opportunity to travel to Italy to do a cooking externship. It was my first time traveling internationally. I was so nervous, but at that point, I had nothing to lose. I kept busy so I wouldn't talk myself out of going, and it worked up until the day I had to leave. As soon as I sat down on the plane, tears started rolling down my face and I couldn't stop. I cried so much that by the time I got to the where

I was staying my head was stopped up like a balloon. Once I got over the fear of being in a new country by myself, it was a beautiful experience. I probably thanked God every minute of the day while I was there because everything I saw was just amazing to me! I couldn't even capture its beauty with a picture.

I was so grateful to be there, grateful for peace and rest, but even amid all that beauty and grace I still couldn't escape my memories. I was extremely excited to have made it there and felt like I earned it, but I still felt sad that Nita, Grandma, nor MeMa could see me there. Italy was the first stop on my journey to healing. But in true fashion for every win, there will be a loss. Returning from Italy, I was met with loss from the moment I stepped off the plane. They lost my luggage at the airport, and once I got in the car my auntie told me there was a bad storm while I was gone. The basement flooded and ruined all my things. I looked at her and just said, "It's okay." I was still on a natural high from Italy. I wasn't going to allow myself to feel any stress or pain at that moment.

I was staying in my aunt's basement before I left for Italy. I didn't have much but a computer and some clothes. It was everything I had left, but it was okay because I had lost more than that before. I went back to my routine, working at the restaurant by day and Target by night. I thought things would be different for me professionally once I got back. I had acquired a new set of skills and added a major boost to my resume, but things did not take off for me like I thought they would. In addition to the stagnation in my career, I was dealing with drama in my personal life as well. I had been in a bad on-again, off relationship with an abusive partner. He had hit me twice before. I would leave him alone, and he would make up for it with gifts and I would talk to him again.

During my last semester of culinary school, we were on again and things were going fine until one night he just snapped. We planned to go out on a date because he constantly complained that I was always with my girls and never kicked it with him. We were supposed to meet up that night for drinks and then go to a movie and chill. I sat at the bar waiting for him, and when I would call to see where he was, he kept saying he was on the way. After a while, he stopped answering the phone altogether, so I left. I drove by his house and he wasn't home. After several attempts to call with no answer, I went home. I decided I would give him a taste of his own medicine. I put my phone on silent, and I parked my car around the corner so he could think I was gone. Well, that little taste of payback quickly escalated into full-on crazy! I had not answered the phone for him. I would always eventually pick up but this time I didn't, and he went into a rage. He slashed all 4 of my tires that night and came back the next morning and keyed my car. He texted me every time he slashed a tire and the next morning when I went out to check my car, he was waiting down the street. He came racing down the street, screaming, and threatening to hurt me and when he couldn't get to me, he texted me threats and told me that he would kill me and bury me next to my mother.

After that blowup, we were off again. He paid for my tires and apologized over and over, but I was tired and fed up. I knew that if I didn't get away it would be either him or me, so I stayed away. However, that didn't last long. He begged me to see him, even cried. I never had a person beg for me or cry, so I let my guard down and let him back in, but it was on very limited terms. I spent a lot of time working during that time. My cooking career was going nowhere, my car was stolen, and every time I looked around, it felt as if I was losing somewhere. I don't know if it was grace or numbness, but I knew something had to give.

My godsister called me to tell me about her engagement and wanted me to be in her wedding in October of 2012. After telling her about all the drama I had been going through, she suggested that I return home to Memphis. I went down for her first bridesmaid's meeting, and I checked on some jobs while I was there. I put in a transfer with my job, and I let things take place. Then, my on-again, off-again friend went to jail. Before he left, he had given me an ultimatum to either choose him or my family. My brother had been talking to me about moving to Chicago with me. I decided that was going to be my chance to choose me. While at work one night, they called me in the office and told me that my transfer went through, so I hit the ground running to prepare for my relocation. In preparing for my move an old classmate from Memphis sent me a message on social media saying that he was living in Chicago and wanted to link up. We spoke over the phone a few times but never hung out. We talked about me moving back to Memphis and he offered to ride with me to help me move. I didn't have anything prepped to go, and at the last minute, my friends and I literally packed up everything I had; me, my stuff, and my problems, and I moved back to Memphis.

Back to Life: Discovery and Healing

No matter how far you travel, you can never escape you. I now know that God took me back to Memphis to heal me. However, the journey to healing was everything but easy. I had so many mixed emotions going back. I knew I needed something to happen, but in my mind, I "settled" on Memphis because, although it was a hurtful place, it was familiar. I had a love-hate/relationship with the city because my most hurtful experiences happened there. I had made it out! I had gone farther than I had ever imagined I would, made other people proud of me, and I finally felt good enough and accomplished.

Returning felt like a failure. Little did I know then, it wouldn't be my only defeat.

I got to Memphis in March 2011 and by July, I was pregnant by that old classmate that volunteered to help me move. One of the first lessons I learned on that new journey was to be very careful with my words. I would always say, "If I don't have a baby by the time I'm 30, I am not having any!" Sure enough, one week before my 30th birthday I found out I was pregnant. Everyone was disappointed in me, even me, but I could not get rid of my baby. I had been wanting a child for a while and I could never get pregnant. When I was in college, I was diagnosed with Polycystic Ovarian Syndrome (PCOS). My doctor told me that it would be harder for me than most women to get pregnant and that I would likely have to take fertility treatments to conceive. With all of that in the back of my mind, finding out that I was pregnant was a joy for me even though the situation was not ideal. I was excited, nervous, and sad at the same time.

The family was telling me to have an abortion, and I questioned myself. I was finding out new information about the father of my child that were screaming signs that I should not have this baby. But deep down inside, I wanted to keep it. Three or so years before though, I'd had a very vivid dream about a baby girl laying in the bed with black hair, but all I could see was hair... never her face. A part of me thought this was the baby from my dream but the other part didn't want it to be true because of my very complicated reality. I wasn't a teenager; I had two jobs, and the reality was the dad neither wanted nor needed another child. I made the decision that I would do what I needed to do and keep my baby.

My pregnancy was easy, but not perfect. Easy because I was not sick a lot and I worked the whole time, but I was truly depressed. My relationship with my growing child's father was horrible. We argued all the time, and things even turned physical when I was three months pregnant resulting in a restraining order and court dates that were later dismissed. After that, I had an appointment to see the doctor for an ultrasound, and during that appointment the doctor said that he was sending me out to a specialist for a closer look because it appeared the baby's arm was broken. That was the beginning of a roller coaster of emotions dealing with this pregnancy. At the second ultrasound appointment, the doctor discovered that it was not a broken arm but a hole in her heart! That news sent me into a panic, and my mind started thinking all types of things: What did I do wrong? Was it from the fight? Is the baby going to survive?

My sleep was off; I just could not rest! I was working during the day and was enrolled in two classes a week at night. After class one night, I spoke to an older classmate who was a pastor. I told him what was going on with me, and he told me his testimony about when he was a baby and the doctors didn't expect him to live. He gave me some oil and told me to put it on my belly every day in the shape of a cross and he said, "You pray over your baby, and God will heal." That conversation gave me peace, but I was still unsure. I grew up in the church all my life, straight Missionary Baptist, but I had never in my life prayed with oil. I was skeptical about using it because it was foreign to me, so I didn't start using it right away. At that point, I felt like I would try anything if it meant healing my baby.

At yet another ultrasound appointment the doctor told me that some babies with a hole in their heart may also have Down Syndrome and advised me to get my amniotic fluid tested, which required getting my stomach stuck with a long needle that could damage, and in extreme cases, kill the baby. As I tried to go numb, my mind filled with "what if's, maybe's, and to do's." That same day I got a package in the mail from one of my really good friends and it was some oil. I decided to take a chance on oil. I put it on my finger, made a cross on my belly, prayed over my baby, and went to bed. The next day I called my aunt and I told her about what the specialist said. She asked me if I was going to have the test done, and I told her I wasn't. At that point, I decided to put it in God's hands. If my baby was going to be born with a disorder then there was nothing I could do about it until she was born, so I was not going to worry about it moment sooner. Releasing my inhibition about the oil and incorporating it into my prayer was the first step for me in truly trusting God, and I finally embraced pregnancy.

Every day I prayed for a healthy, happy baby and experienced the rest of my pregnancy with grace. My original due date was March 30th, so I set my maternity leave date to start the week before on Saturday, March 24th. My boss sent me home a little early that day and told me to get started on my leave. When I got home, I talked on the phone with my cousin and godsister. I hung up the phone and my water broke! We arrived at the hospital at about 2 p.m. and the next morning, my beautiful baby girl was born at 1:59 a.m. Sunday the 25th of March. 6lbs 7oz, and as perfect as a baby could be! She was beautiful; she came out with a head full of hair, ten fingers, and ten toes.

I gave her my grandmother and mother's middle name, Christine Monae. She was born two days after my grandmother's birthday and two days before my grandfather's birthday. I barely had time to see her before they whisked her away to the NICU, which made me sad. But I was in love. And after delivery, I was transferred to another room. My godsister and Christine's aunt were in the room with me during the birth. Christine's aunt told me that Christine's father said he was coming but never showed up. Other than the pictures I sent him, it was a week before he saw her. After I got to the other room, I just laid in the bed and cried. I had never felt so alone in my life; I missed my Momma and Grandma. All my friends were in Chicago, and Christine's dad was nowhere to be found, so I cried some more until I cried myself to sleep.

Despite my loneliness, I was completely in love with Christine, and I was so grateful for her. No Down Syndrome, no broken bones, just a happy baby. She did struggle with her heart and would later need to undergo surgery at three months. Life with my new baby was very different. I thought that I was prepared because I used to help my mom with my brother and I babysat all the time for family and friends, but nothing prepares for a child more than having your own. I was always watching her sleep and putting my finger under her nose to make sure she was still breathing. She struggled to breathe, and the doctors told me to monitor her during the night. She had a lot of doctor's appointments leading up to her surgery, and the doctors made sure she was gaining enough weight to be ready for her surgery.

When Christine turned three months, the doctor decided that she had gained enough weight to withstand the surgery and set her surgery date for the Tuesday after Father's Day. That Sunday we planned to get Christine "blessed" at church. During the service, the pastor called us up for the prayer and told the church he why he was praying for my baby and what her situation was. Before he prayed, he began to address me spiritually or, as church folks would say, prophecy. He told me that although this was surgery to repair her heart, it would be healing for mine. He told me that I struggled with self-confidence. His words pierced, and I broke down for a moment. Even though I felt it at that moment, it would be a year and a half before I would even begin to understand. In my opinion, prophecies are given to us for three reasons: conformation, correction, or contingency, and mine was a contingency plan.

My Wilderness Year

Life after Christine's surgery was a roller coaster, to say the least. A year after dealing with Christine's surgery, I found myself in the hospital having my own. I was in the hospital for a week having to have my gallbladder removed. After dealing with her surgery and recovery, my surgery and recovery, work, and school, I was exhausted and overwhelmed. I didn't have a handle on things like I thought I did and, honestly, I didn't know what to do. I couldn't explain to anyone what I was feeling, so I went back to my favorite place: numb.

This time I was convinced that I would stay there, so the "now and then" weed-smoking I would do quickly became a habit. I was smoking almost every day after I picked Christine up from daycare and got home. I just wanted not to feel any emotions, or pain I just wanted my mind and my body to be numb. I went through so many different emotions when it came to Christine. I constantly compared my life to my mom's out of fear that I was making the same mistakes. I even called her godmother and asked her to take Christine away from me because every day I would pick her up from daycare she would be so excited and happy to see me, and that terrified me because I was the same way about my momma and the thought of me disappointing her or causing her pain would kill me.

I had always wanted to be a mother and I wanted Christine's love and I wanted her to love me, but at that moment I just didn't feel like I had enough in me to do it. In 2 Corinthians 12, Paul was given a thorn in his side by God. Three times Paul begged God to take it away from and God simply answered, "My grace is sufficient for thee: for my power works best in weakness." During this time, I was broken and weak, but God never breaks his promises. Just as his word said, his power took hold of my weakness. After the roller coaster year of a ride that I had, I was looking forward to celebrating the holidays. The day after Christmas we flew out to Chicago for a couple of days to spend time with my sister and her husband. On the way to the airport, I sent this message out to three of my close friends as encouragement for going into the new year.

Dec 30, 2013, 5:29 AM

This year we need to spend time listening to God to find our ministry. All of us are strong, driven, talented women, and God connected us for a purpose. It is a reason now that he has moved us all to an uneasy, unsettled point in our lives. It's time for a change. Our challenge this year is to remove self and replace it with God. He is preparing us for the next level, and we need to be ready. So as my sister and my friend, this is our challenge for 2014:

1. TRUST God for everything.
2. Listen to God before I make a decision.
3. Continue to keep each other lifted
4. Hold me accountable, and I will you.
5. Live without fear.

This is my promise to God, myself, and my sisters. I love you guys more than you know, and we are going to have a great 2014!

2014 was the real beginning of my discovery; I like to call it my wilderness year. After receiving that word from my pastor two years before, I was finally starting to do the repairs I needed to my heart. At the time, I had no idea how this message would change the course of my life. The one thing that you must learn about God is that where there is a challenge, there will always be a test. Knowing the difference between the two seems easy, but when you are going through, they both can be difficult. When I sent that message, I was making a declaration that at the time sounded great, but I still had to do the work it would take to put action to those words. That was the test. The first thing on the challenge was to trust God with everything. That was a lesson and a test rolled up in one because the first thing I learned was to be careful with my words. I had said everything, and that meant EVERYTHING, not just the stuff I wanted God to see and hold on to; the things I thought I could handle on my own. With that statement, the test began.

Things were quiet at first. That little break in Chicago did me good, and I was ready to face 2014 with a brand new perspective. I was finishing up my classes at school and work was going the same, and with all that my plate was full. Christine turned three, and we had a big party at the house for her. Even her dad and I were getting along. A few months after the party, I was enrolled in this non-profit class that teaches you about saving and homeownership. During this class, the Nita Joe Project came to life and the next 63 days would challenge and test me in ways I could never imagine. I call this time my wilderness time because during these 63 days I was praying and fasting. As the parts of the Nita Joe Project were unfolded, I was tested on every hand.

On May 3, 2014 my dad died seventeen years and one day after my mom. I was not sure how to feel, so I went to my most comfortable place and that was numb. We did not have the best relationship, but it was fairly new. I had only seen him one time when I was a child, at age three or four, because he had been locked up most of my life and when he finally got out the next time I saw him I was twenty-eight. Most of my communication with him over the years was through letters. I had made up an idea of him in my head for years. I had imagined him as our way out, especially during the time my mom was going through her changes. I used to sit outside and daydream that he would come around the corner in a limo and take us out of that place. I spent years writing to him, asking him questions, and searching for my brothers and sisters. He had gotten out of jail and into a halfway house during my senior year of high school, and by my senior year of college he was out and we started a relationship just talking on the phone.

The first time I saw him as an adult, I was twenty-eight years old, and he had sent me an invitation to him and his wife's 50th wedding anniversary party. At that moment, I realized I was an outside kid. When I got there, we talked, and we had a very real conversation about my mom. He told me, "I am not going to apologize for the past, all we are going to do is move forward," so we did. After my visit, I was certain of who he was, and I finally killed the fantasy in my head. We kept in touch over the years and he would call and give me advice after Christine was born. Ironically, he died from the same heart condition that Christine was born with, and finding out this news made my pastor's prophecy clearer. Although I was sad and felt like a true orphan, at the same time I felt free. The next 42 days of the fast were easier but challenging. This project was unfolding faster than I had imagined. As God reviled more and more of this project to me, it was clear and evident that this healing was not about just helping others. It was my plan for me to get free.

Phase 1: The Cleanse

Cleanse

/klenz/

Verb

- to make (something, especially the skin) thoroughly clean.
- to rid (a person, place, or thing) of something seen as unpleasant, unwanted, or defiling.
- to free (someone) from a sin or guilt.

The Cleanse Phase is designed to help break down some of the barriers that hold us hostage and things that stunt our growth and to expose any hindrances that keep us from getting to where God wants us to be. We want to expose these ugly truths about ourselves to learn ourselves inside and out and take the first steps to freedom. Although this phase is called The Cleanse, it requires you to get deep, down, and dirty with your soul.

How do I prepare for my cleanse?

According to Dr. Mark Hyman's Detox Made Simple, there are five steps to prepare your body for detox: make a list, journal, gather supplements, exercise, and rest.

Here is The Nita Joe Project's version:

Make a List

And the Lord answered me, and said write the vision, and make it plain on tables, that he may run that reads it. For the vision is yet for an appointed time, but at the end, it shall speak, and not lie though it tarry, wait for it; because it will surely come, it will not tarry. **Habakkuk 2:2-3**

Sit down and write down all of the things that you feel are hindrances in your life. Be raw and honest with yourself, and make sure it's not just surface stuff. You want to speak to those things that only God sees. Organize and prioritize the things that you want God to remove or work on and develop a plan of action. Make sure to allow yourself a realistic timeframe to release and heal.

Journal

Trust in him at all time; ye people, pour out your heart before him: God is a refuge for us. **Psalms 62:8**

Put it all on the line (literally) and write your release date! Formulate an outlet for your healing to begin. Read it and compare it to the things on your list and begin to check them off as God takes you through them.

Gather Any Supplements

Pray without ceasing. In everything give thanks: for this is the will of God in Christ Jesus concerning you. 1 Thessalonians 5:17-18

Surround yourself with positive things. Saturate yourself with the things that increase your awareness of God. Train your ear to hear God's voice, because now you are exposed, and you must be okay with being naked! The moment you decide to make a positive change in your life, that is when the real challenge begins.

Exercise

This book of the law shall not depart out of your mouth; but you shall meditate therein day and night' that you may observe to do according to all that is written therein: for then you shall make your way prosperous, and then you shall have good success. Joshua 1:8-9

Challenge your mind with reading and listening. Finding a good devotional, inspirational song, or listening to a sermon will help guide you on your walk. Then exercise your mouth to speak the knowledge you have learned. Exercise your body by walking in your new truth as you become more comfortable with being naked! Believe, praise, trust, and serve.

Rest

Let us lay aside every weight, and the sin which does so easily beset us, and let us run with patience the race that is set before us, looking to Jesus the author and finisher of our faith. Hebrews 12:1

Dr. Mark Harmon states, "Detoxification requires you to slow down." As God begins to release and unravel the things that have bound you up and held you hostage, you will begin to feel weak. During this time, it is very important to be still! Make time to have a one on one session with God; lay still, be quiet, and listen to him whisper to you. Let him renew your spirit so that you can strengthen yourself for your journey ahead.

Phase II: Restoration and Implantation

Congratulations, you made it through your first phase!

For the last 21 days you have purged, cried, prayed, doubted, cried some more, and prayed again. It may have been tough, but you are still here! Now you are empty. You laid it all out before God and you are probably wondering what's next? Don't worry, all of it was and is necessary. You needed to be empty for God to fill you back up and make you new.

God will always give provisions for your future. Even if you lose some things along the way, you will often find that you still have everything you need. I must admit, throughout my journey, I have been blessed to have some extraordinary women in my life. Women who taught me things that were essential to becoming a woman. As a child, I spent a lot of time with my great grandmothers and my godmother's grandmom. At age seven, MeMa sat me down, put the ironing board low enough for me to reach, pulled out my clothes, and taught me how to iron. Next, she showed me how to sew on a button and sew up a hole. Before each lesson, she would say, "You need to learn how to do this because I won't be around always." MeMa lost her mother at eight years old and these were lessons she learned early on.

Grand taught me the importance of education. She was a retired teacher, and I spent many nights learning math facts with popsicle sticks or toothpicks at her kitchen table. Grand also taught me how to appreciate music, as I was a faithful member of her angel choir. During the summer months, I learned gardening at Mama Sadie's house. Mama Sadie was my grandfather's mother. At her house, I was in charge of pulling weeds out of the garden. I had my first laundry lesson there. Mama Sadie never owned a washer and dryer. She used a washboard in the bathtub, and I would help her hang the clothes out on the line. In addition to my early lessons, later when I was in Chicago, my aunt taught me a very important rule for housekeeping: everything has a place. Their lessons not only taught me a skill, but they also taught me about survival and perseverance.

It is important to understand that some lessons are taught, and other lessons come from an experience.

Only one time in my life can I remember my whole family going to church together. My uncle, Clarence, was having something at the church he played for and MeMa wanted us all to be there. I was so excited by this, because we were going to all be together; it felt like it was Christmas. Grandma and Nita had on matching dresses and wedding vein hats. We walked in the church looking like a million bucks and sat on the third row from the front. I was on top of the world all through service until we got to communion. As we passed the communion plate down the row, everyone took their cracker and wine except Nita. When she let the plate pass her, I leaned over and whispered, "Why didn't you take communion?" She paused for a moment, looked at me, and whispered back, "Because I'm not living right." I often wondered who told her that, or where she learned that type of punishment from God. I felt sad because I was young and I thought that God was mad at her, but now it seems like that was learned punishment.

It wasn't until I was in her shoes that I understood why she refused communion. I was sitting in church, my body was sore, and the inside of my lip was blue and bruised from fighting with my daughter's dad. I was sitting in the place for healing, feeling unloved, broken, and ashamed of myself. I wanted to hide from God because I was ashamed, and taking communion seemed wrong. Sometimes the hardest person to forgive is yourself. Yes, you may have made some mistakes, you may have repeated them, and you will most likely make a few more. What is important to know is that God is merciful and forgiving. Don't continue to hold yourself hostage for things God has already forgiven you for. Deciding to trust God every day is hard, and change can be even harder, but staying in your comfort zone can stunt your growth. Don't let life as you always known it handcuff you into stagnation. This is where you take control.

The Restoration and Implantation Phase is broken down into two parts because, as mentioned before, results are not cookie cutter. Both portions of this phase are essential to progression into Phase III. The cleanse may have broken you down, but these 21days are all about you! Self-care and self-investment will be your focus. Taking the time to learn yourself, love yourself, and set yourself free.

Restoration

Restoration

/ˌrestəˈrāSH(ə)n/

Noun

- the action of returning something to a former owner, place, or condition.

Restore to me the joy of your salvation; and uphold me with your free spirit. Psalms 51:12

The Restoration Phase causes you to take account of where you are now and plan for where you want to be. You have cleansed and purged, but there may have been a few things you have lost or neglected that you want to restore and bring with you along your journey to the new you. During our season of bondage, things like our health, finances, and appearance can be neglected. Before we learned to take control of our peace, we may have turned to self-destructive vices. Over time, those coping mechanisms can abuse our bodies. Whether married or single, being well mentally and physically is important to properly run your household. A part of your healing and restoration is being healthy inside and out. As you are on your journey to freedom, take time to love yourself. Be good to your body and take control of your health. Our finances are another thing that may need restoration. Being good stewards of our bodies and our money reduces worry and stress that can disrupt our healing. Seeking guidance and continuing to educate ourselves will help us relearn some things we already may know and make room for us to learn the things we don't.

Implantation

Implantation
/ˌimplanˈtāSH(ə)n/
Noun

- the action of implanting or state of being implanted.

For I am about to do something new. See, I have already begun! Do you not see it? I will make a pathway through the wilderness. I will create rivers in the dry wasteland. Isaiah 43:19

As women, we relate implantation to pregnancy. However, in this project, we relate implantation to receiving and learning something new. Devotion, Service, and Partnership will help the "new you" post-cleanse.

Devotion

Your word is a lamp to my feet and light to my path. Psalms 119:105

You can control most situations in life by first controlling yourself. Somewhere along the way, someone taught us that there was strength in worrying and joy only comes after suffering. It is possible to be happy without sorrow. It's called peace. You have to make your peace intentional by taking time daily to get in the presence of God. Some may call it meditation, others may call it prayer, either way, making time to "tune in" with God can set the course of your day. Daily devotion is important because it can clean your mind and command your day. Every time God blesses us with a new day, it is a new chance to make that day better than the day before. Spending time in devotion gives you a place to release, think, and create. Devotion is the blueprint on how to maintain your peace when going back out in the world.

Service

As each has received a gift, use it to serve one another, as good stewards of God's varied grace: whoever speaks, as one who speaks. **1 Peter 4:10**

I know what you are thinking, "What does service have to do with me getting to freedom?" Although it may seem unrelated, you can find healing, peace, and clarity in your service to others. When you serve others, you get to see life beyond yourself. Things done in service are teachable moments that open your mind and heart to the blessings of God. Service can also allow you to place yourself in someone else's shoes and it teaches humility. In my opinion, the most powerful story of service in the Bible was the last supper. Jesus, in all his glory with the fate of the world on his shoulders and facing betrayal from a brother, served. He put aside all of his burdens to wash the disciple's feet. Though the lesson in this story emphasizes humility and service, Jesus was also teaching accountability. There is healing and opportunity in service; serve free.

Partnership

***Iron sharpens iron and one man sharpens another.*
Proverbs 27:17**

Having a good support system is the most important part of this project. Even though this journey is personal, you don't have to go alone. Having friends and family around you that pray with, and for, you and who encourage and push you to better you, helps make this difficult journey a little easier. Having an accountability partner builds your faith and trust. Partnership builds the confidence that will unlock the door to your freedom. Go ahead and walk in; you are almost there!

Freedom

/ˈfrēdəm/

Noun

- the power or right to act, speak, or think as one wants without hindrance or restraint.
- the state of not being imprisoned or enslaved.

Stand fast therefore in the liberty with which Christ has made us free and be not entangled again with the yoke of bondage. Galatians 5:1

Welcome to your final phase!

Give yourself a round of applause. I want you to know I am proud of you! I'm sure that it has been an interesting 42 days. For one month, one week, and four days you have been on a rollercoaster ride of emotion that has broken you down and built you back up. You could have given up after all of that, but you made it and now it is time to set you free! The Freedom Phase is a bit of a continuation of Phase II; however, it is not as intensive. In Phase III you take the majority of the responsibility for your deliverance.

I have never had a time in my life that didn't include people and problems, and I crave to be free! I crave to live unapologetically and know without a doubt who I am and who I am supposed to be. For years, I wasted time trying to be whomever I thought everyone else wanted me to be. Shrinking to fit because I never felt like I belonged…anywhere. I was so far from where I was, but still unsure of where I was going. All I was sure of was that I wanted to be free. When you lose so much, sometimes you hold on to the wrong things just to say you have something to hold on to. My fear of being left with nothing clouded my vision, and I never stopped to think that maybe God's plan was for me to lose it all.

For six years, I was in a tug-a-war with my freedom. Pulling it in close when it was comfortable, and letting it go when it got too hard. I was telling God I was all in with my heart, but my mind wouldn't let me be free. Even though Nita was long gone, she was free and I was holding her captive and calling it protection because I was afraid of being me. If my fight and sacrifices were truly all for Nita's honor, then I couldn't be afraid to let her go and set myself free. I had to learn that freedom is a process of progression. I had to learn that freedom, just like love, is a decision. So I decided to be free! I lay my life on these lines as living proof of a finite example of God's infinite capabilities. Freedom is yours; take it, live it, and share it with others. You never know how your journey will help set someone free!

Did you know that there are levels of freedom? One would argue that you are either free or captive with no gray areas to debate. However, the gray areas are, in fact, the very things that blocked us in the first place. Yes, it is true that if you are not being held captive physically, you are free; but are you free indeed? With all the cleaning, restoration, and implantation you have done, you are no longer a slave to vices; but are you free in your truth?

The mother of freedom is truth. It may take the experience for some or a journey for others. No matter how you get there, as long as you seek the truth, freedom will always come through. Sometimes seeking the truth can be hard and living it can be dangerous, but it is better to live in freedom with the truth than live the rest of your life a prisoner to lies. People who say the truth hurts have not yet experienced the freedom that truth affords you. Knowing the truth and living the truth are two very different things. To know your truth is to accept the good and the bad of your reality but not act on it. Living your truth is accepting the good and the bad of your reality and forgiving yourself and others regardless of fault. God's word, the Bible, is our manual to being free indeed. To maintain and manage your freedom, you have to have guidance, motives, and encouragement that promotes you being free! To be free indeed, let the truth be your shield so that no one can use it as a weapon against you.

In Phase I & II, you learned that gathering supplements and doing devotion is an important part of your journey. In the Freedom Phase, scriptures can provide the guidance you need to help you manage your peace and maintain your freedom.

Daily Victories

Therefore, do not worry about tomorrow for tomorrow will worry about itself. Each day has enough trouble of its own. **Matthew 6:34**

To maintain freedom, you must experience a victory each day. Set a goal for your day during your morning devotion and make that the focus of your day. Placing that accountability on yourself pushes you to reach that goal, and when you do... celebrate it! During your nightly reflection, seal your victory with praise by thanking God for an abundance of chances. You'll find your rest will be better when you have victories each day.

Share the Load

Being confident of this, that he who began a good work in you will carry it on to completion until the day of Christ Jesus. **Philippians 1:6**

God gifted women with a different type of strength. With that strength comes the natural propensity to "carry." We carry babies, purses, bags, and sometimes weight. With all the things we physically carry daily, it tends to be second nature for us to carry things internally as well. Our strength is so natural and so well suited that sometimes we forget that we don't have to carry it all. Share the load. God knows you better than you know yourself, so don't be afraid to give things over to him. If you want to continue to be free, you have to know when to ask for help. God never promised us a life without pain or frustration, but he did promise never to leave or forsake you. Remember, even though you are free, life doesn't stop. Keep going! God always finishes what he starts. Lighten up.

Be Box Free

Do not be conformed to this world, but be transformed by the renewal of your mind, that by testing you may discern what is the will of God, what is good and acceptable and perfect. Romans 8:12-2

Freedom requires you to think outside the box. We can't put God in a box, so if we are his children we have to learn how to live box free. Living box free is realizing that God is an experience, God is everywhere, and God is in everything. You have to take time to experience God differently. Sometimes you need to just go outside and experience God and all his glory. Let the sun give you a warm hug, let the breeze blow away your tears, let the birds sing you a song, and let the trees show you how to dance. It sounds silly, but getting that experience from the simple things we take for granted every day will help you further understand who God is. Freedom looks different for everyone. Be open to new experiences and open your mind to new expectations. Honor God by trusting him to push you beyond your limits; that is the best way to be box free.

Graduation Day

At every commencement program, there is a speaker who gives a speech to inspire the graduates to do great things in their next stage of life. Now that you made it to the end of The Nita Joe Project, it's time to go back out into the world and be free. Today, I will be your guest speaker. I don't have a long profound speech, but I do have two things I want to give you to take with you on your way. I want to give you a scripture to keep in your heart and an affirmation to keep in your spirit.

For you know the plans I have for you declares the Lord, plans to prosper you and not harm you, plans to give you hope and a future. Jeremiah 29:11

Keep this scripture in your heart and, on the days when freedom gets hard, it will help make things a little easier to bear. Remember, your pain has a purpose!

Affirmation: I will no longer shrink to fit! I serve a God that is high and lifted up far beyond the heavens, and that is where my thoughts should be. I will not put limits and boundaries on a limitless God! I will no longer place myself in a box designed to please others, but I will reach down to bring them to a high level. Greatness is only the beginning. Today, I am free to be everything God designed me to be!

Every day you go out in the world, affirm yourself and be confident in your freedom. As you continue to grow in freedom, your affirmations will change, but remember to be encouraged no matter what life brings.

It's graduation day! You made it, now go be free

Website: www.nadonnagaryauthor.com
Facebook: NaDonna Gary, Author
Instagram: @nadonnagary.author
Twitter: @AuthorNGary1

Creative Control With Self-Publishing

Divine Legacy Publishing provides authors with the guid-ance necessary to take creative control of their work through self-publishing. We provide:

Writing Coaching

Professional Editing

Author Branding

Self-Publishing Coaching

Graphic Design

Website Design

Let Divine Legacy Publishing help you master the business of self-publishing.

Made in the USA
Columbia, SC
29 June 2021

41019283R00046